Little Nellie
of
Holy God

1903-1908

By
Sister Mary Dominic, R.G.S.

Pictures by
Sister M. John Vianney, S.S.N.D.

TAN BOOKS AND PUBLISHERS, INC.
Rockford, Illinois 61105

Copyright © 1961 by The Bruce Publishing Company, Milwaukee, Wisconsin.

Retypeset and republished by TAN Books and Publishers, Inc. in 2006, with many minor adjustments to text and illustrations. These editorial changes copyright © 2006 by TAN Books and Publishers, Inc.

ISBN 0-89555-834-3

Printed and bound in the United States of America.

TAN BOOKS AND PUBLISHERS, INC.
P.O. Box 424
Rockford, Illinois 61105
2006

Dedicated to
Mother M. Francis Xavier,
who told me about
Little Nellie of Holy God.

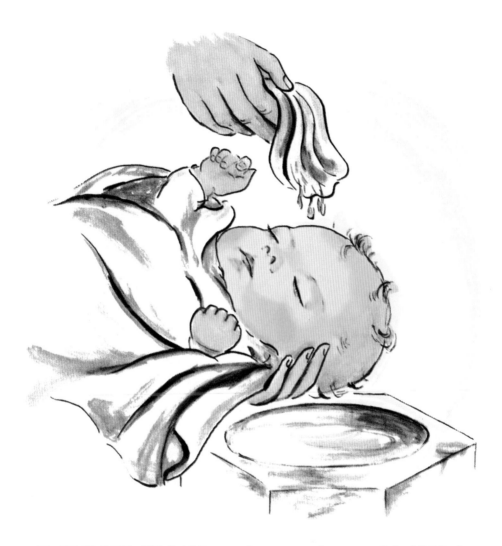

NELLIE ORGAN was born on August 24, 1903, in Ireland. Her father was a soldier, and her mother lived with him in a military barracks. Just a few days after Nellie was born, she was baptized. Through that Baptism, little Nellie Organ became a child of God.*

---

* Nellie's baptismal name was Ellen. —*Publisher*, 2006.

Nellie's mother often brought her down to the seashore. She sat on the golden sand to make big sand castles for Nellie. There she talked to her about God and told her all sorts of wonderful things about Him. Nellie learned to say the Rosary with her mother.

When only two, Nellie would toddle off to Mass with her soldier-father. All along the way she prattled about *Holy God.* That was the only way she ever spoke of God. Nobody knows where she learned to call Him that.

One day, Nellie's mother became ill. A babysitter took care of Nellie. She dropped the baby, but she did not tell anyone. Nellie's hip and back were twisted out of joint. As the little arms and legs grew, the trouble became painful, but Nellie did not know how to tell anyone.

When Nellie was three years old, the Angels came for Mrs. Organ and took her up to Heaven.

Nellie was glad that her Mama was in Heaven with Holy God and Blessed Mother Mary and the Angels, but she was lonesome too. Nellie's back hurt her, but she could not explain this, so she just cried.

A Good Shepherd Home was close to the barracks. Private Organ went there to visit one day. He thought that Nellie and her sister would be happy with the Good Shepherd Sisters. The Sisters wanted to take good care of Nellie because she did not have any mother. Nellie was happy at the Good Shepherd and she called all the Sisters "Mothers."

The Sisters learned that Nellie had a bad temper. When she got angry, she would stomp her little feet and fire would seem to flash from her big, dark eyes. Like every child, she had to try every day to make up for her faults.

Sometimes Nellie was a naughty little girl. One time she kept five or six girls late for supper. But afterward she was sorry and she made an Act of Contrition. She said, "Holy God, I am very sorry for keeping the girls late for supper. Please forgive me and make me a good child and bless me and my Mothers."

Nellie could not walk well. The Sisters bought her special slippers with rose-colored socks. Nellie was very fond of her pretty shoes and socks.

One day Nellie stopped before a statue of the Holy Infant. "Jesus," she said, "if You give me Your ball, I will give You my little shoes."

"Oh, Nellie," said her nurse, "you cannot have that."

"He can give it to me if He likes," Nellie replied, and she was right. But Jesus did not give her His little ball. He gave her suffering instead.

One day her nurse took Nellie along to make the Stations of the Cross. Nellie could not understand why Holy God let Himself be nailed to the Cross. She asked, "But why does He let them do that? He could stop them if He liked."

The nurse told her that Jesus wanted to suffer and die for our sins. Nellie burst into tears, crying over and over, "Poor Holy God! Oh, poor Holy God."

One day Nellie swallowed some red and yellow beads. They stuck in her throat. The doctor came to take them out. Then he gave Nellie a check-up. He said that Nellie was getting very sick, just like her mother, and that she could not live for even one more year.

The Bishop gave Nellie Confirmation.

Nellie said, "I am now the little soldier of Holy God."
She stopped being a crybaby, and she tried never to
lose her temper again.

Nellie longed for Holy God. She wanted to receive Him in Holy Communion. But in those days, children could not receive Jesus until they were twelve years old, and Nellie was only four. She used to lie quietly in her little bed, whispering over and over to herself, "Oh, I am longing for Holy God! I wonder when He will come. I would like to have Him in my heart."

"Mother," she whispered to her nurse one morning, "when you get Holy God in the chapel, will you come back and kiss me? Then you can go back to the chapel again."

One day the Blessed Sacrament was exposed on the altar. The nurse carried Nellie down to the chapel. It was the first time she had ever seen the monstrance. With her eyes glued on it, she whispered: "There He is! There is Holy God now!" From then on, Nellie always knew when there was Exposition of the Blessed Sacrament. "Holy God is not locked up today," she would say. "Take me down. I want to talk to Him." Nobody knew how she knew.

Baby Jesus knew that Nellie was tired of lying in a little bed alone all day long, so He used to do kind deeds for her. One day He gave her a flower. Another time He danced for her. Occasionally He visited and talked to her.

A holy priest came to see Nellie. "What is Holy Communion?" he asked her.

"It is Holy God," she answered. "It is He who makes the nuns and everybody else holy."

The priest said he would ask the Bishop's permission for Nellie's First Communion even though she was only four years and three months old.

Long before the sun got up on her First Communion morning, Nellie lay wide awake.

The Sisters dressed her all in white, and seated her on a little easy chair before the altar.

Then Father Bury brought Jesus to His Little Lover, Nellie of Holy God. A beautiful light lit up her little face. Nellie quietly thanked her wonderful Holy God.

Nellie received Holy God many times after that first Communion. Every time, that beautiful light shone from her face. Many people saw this heavenly light glowing after Holy Communion.

Sometimes after Holy Communion, Nellie lay quite still for hours, wanting nothing. Although she was hot and burning with fever, she never thought of a drink during these hours of silent thanksgiving prayer.

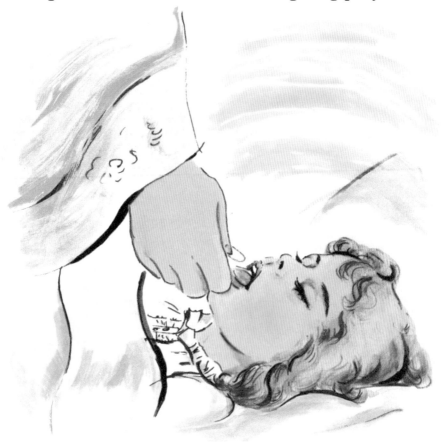

One day Nellie said to her nurse, "Mother, sit down there." Then she went on, "Tell me, Mother, how are you feeling today?"

"Very well, Nellie," replied the nurse.

"But tell me, Mother," the child went on, "do you feel you are coming close to Holy God? I do."

Knowing that Little Nellie would soon go to Heaven, Mother Francis said to her, "Please ask Holy God to take me to Heaven with you. I want very much to go."

Nellie shook her head. "Holy God cannot take you, Mother, 'til you are better and do what He wants you to do."

For ninety-nine years Mother Francis did the things that God wanted her to do. In 1960, God took her to Heaven from the Good Shepherd Home in St. Paul, Minnesota.

Nellie was four years and five months old. She had received Holy Communion thirty-two times. She belonged to Our Lady's Sodality and the Apostleship of Prayer. She had been anointed. She had received five of the Seven Sacraments. She was really nearing Holy God; in fact, she was ready to fly into His arms.

Nellie died on a Sunday, Holy God's own day. For about an hour she lay quite still. Her lips moved as though she were speaking. Then, with a beautiful, happy smile, Little Nellie of Holy God died. It was four o'clock, February 2, 1908.

IN
LOVING MEMORY
of
LITTLE NELLIE
of
HOLY GOD
WHO DIED
FEBRUARY 2ND 1908
R.I.P.

In her First Communion dress, wreath and veil, with her silver Sodality medal on a blue ribbon around her neck, Little Nellie was buried. Because so many people were coming to pray at her grave, Little Nellie was brought, one year later, to the Sisters' cemetery. Then it was found that her golden curls had grown a little. The dress, wreath and veil of First Communion in which she had been buried were almost as good as new. Nellie looked as sweet and beautiful as if she had just had a nice, long sleep.

The Holy Father, Pope Pius X, heard of Little Nellie. He was told how she had longed for Jesus in Holy Communion, and how lovingly she had received Him. "There!" he cried. "That is the sign for which I was waiting." A few months later, Pope Pius X said that all little children could make their First Holy Communion.* He asked Little Nellie's Bishop for a relic of her.

The Bishop who had confirmed Nellie and had given permission for her First Holy Communion then approved a prayer for her canonization. St. Pius X wrote that he blessed all who would recommend frequent Communion to little boys and girls. He said that Little Nellie should be their model.

"The Children's Pope"

---

* Decree *Quam Singulari*, 1910. —*Publisher*, 2006.

PRAYER

O JESUS, Divine Friend of little children, we thank Thee for the signal graces Thou didst confer upon Thy holy servant, Little Nellie, by inspiring her with such great devotion to Thy Sacred Passion and such ardent love of Thy Blessed Eucharist.

Grant, we beseech Thee, O Lord, the fulfillment of Thy designs regarding Thy loving little servant, for Thy greater glory and for the sanctification of souls.

We adore Thee, O Jesus, ever present in the Blessed Sacrament; we pray that Thy Sacred Presence may be honored daily more and more; that the little ones, whom Thou desirest to come to Thee, may frequently approach Thy Holy Table.

O Sacrament Most Holy, O Sacrament Divine,
all praise and all thanksgiving
be every moment Thine.

Imprimatur
✠ T. A. O'Callaghan, O.P.
Bishop of Cork

"May God enrich with every blessing Abbé Prevost and all those who recommend frequent Communion to little boys and girls, proposing Nellie as their model."

—Pope St. Pius X
June 4, 1912

Any child who enjoyed Little Nellie of Holy God
will <u>love</u> the Catholic Children's Treasure Box!! . . .

Catholic Children's Treasure Box. *Stories, Poems, Games, Fun Things to Make and Do.* Ages 3-8 and up. Maryknoll Sisters (1950s). Wonderful, full-color series combining fun, innocence and Catholic faith! These books teach children how to be good! Stories include "A Little Girl Named Therese" (St. Therese) in Books 1-6, stories about Wupsy (a Guardian Angel), "The Boy Who Told Lies," etc. For a wide range of ages (preschool through about 10). Children love them! Beautiful pictures!

32 Pp. each. PB. Imprimatur.
10-1/4" x 8-1/4". Full color on every page. ($5.00 each)

No. 1371. Set of Books 1-10. (Reg. $50.00)   **$40.00**
No. 1372. Set of Books 11-20. (Reg. $50.00)   **$40.00**
No. 1374. Set of Books 1-20.   **$80.00**

At your Bookdealer or direct from the Publisher.
TAN BOOKS AND PUBLISHERS, INC.
P.O. Box 424, Rockford, Illinois 61105

Toll Free 1-800-437-5876   Fax 815-226-7770
Tel 815-226-7777   www.tanbooks.com
Prices subject to change.